& ICE

BARENTS SEA

BAFFIN BAY

BALTIC S.

NORTH SEA

CASPIAN S.

BLACK S.

MEDITERRANEAN SEA

PERSIAN GULF

RED SEA

GULF of ADEN

ARABIAN SEA

BAY of BENGAL

ATLANTIC OCEAN

INDIAN OCEAN

BBEAN

OCEAN

the
SEAS & OCEANS
of
the WORLD
COMMONWEALTH of PIRATES

MMV

A THOUSAND YEARS OF

Pirates

WILLIAM GILKERSON TUNDRA BOOKS

This work is dedicated to my treasured captains, Paul Erling Johnson, Daniel Moreland, and Llewellyn Howland III.

Text and illustrations copyright © 2009 by William Gilkerson

Published in Canada by Tundra Books,
75 Sherbourne Street, Toronto, Ontario M5A 2P9

Published in the United States by Tundra Books of Northern New York,
P.O. Box 1030, Plattsburgh, New York 12901

Library of Congress Control Number: 2001012345

Library and Archives Canada Cataloguing in Publication

Gilkerson, William
    A thousand years of pirates / William Gilkerson.
Includes index.
ISBN 978-0-88776-924-5

  1. Pirates-History-Juvenile literature. 2. Piracy-History-Juvenile literature. I. Title.

G535.G54 2009   J910.4'5   C2008-906639-1

We acknowledge the financial support of the Government of Canada through the Book Publishing Industry Development Program (BPIDP) and that of the Government of Ontario through the Ontario Media Development Corporation's Ontario Book Initiative. We further acknowledge the support of the Canada Council for the Arts and the Ontario Arts Council for our publishing program.

ONTARIO ARTS COUNCIL
CONSEIL DES ARTS DE L'ONTARIO

Design: Andrew Roberts

Printed and bound in China

1 2 3 4 5 6   14 13 12 11 10 09

CONTENTS

— 1 —
FROM VIKINGS TO CONQUISTADORES

Pirates have been here from time before memory –

first on the waters of the Aegean Sea four thousand years ago, and later around Africa,

throughout the Orient, off the islands of Indonesia, on the Pacific Ocean, and from

the warm Sea of the Caribs to the wintry fjords of Scandinavia, where this account begins.

It was in Sweden, Denmark, and Norway that Norsemen conceived the ships and the tactics

that would be used by all of the generations of European pirates to follow.

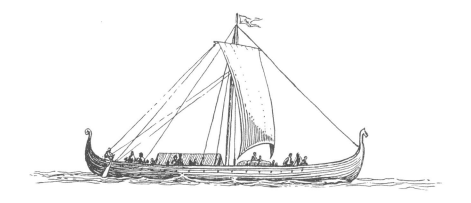

In ancient times, the ancestors of the Vikings learned to split and shape oak trees into planks. These had a natural twist which, when laid opposite, made the shape of a boat. Several planks together, carefully sculpted and fitted by ax to a straight keel-piece and two end-pieces, made a vessel that could carry cargo and enough men to row it. Over the centuries, the beautifully crafted Norse boats evolved into ships that could crisscross all of the northern seas under sail, and then the oceans beyond, reaching even the shores of America, five hundred years before Columbus.

The same axes that shaped the Viking ships became fierce weapons in the hands of determined warriors. Though wooden swords and shields were used for sparring, starting in childhood, the sons of the Norsemen were taught by fathers, uncles, and neighbors to swing an ax at an opponent, or to throw it with deadly accuracy. According to the ancient religion of that place and time, warriors who fell in combat earned a seat for the rest of eternity in the mead halls of Valhalla, home to warlike gods and to mortal heroes slain nobly in battle. Meanwhile, until they met that fate, there was good marauding, trading, and pillaging to reward warriors, far from home.

With their seaworthy ships and characteristic ferocity, the Vikings brought many battles to the coasts of Europe, especially to Scotland, Ireland, and England. In those waters cargo vessels waited to be captured, and there were prosperous settlements to plunder ashore. Although the usual tactic of the Norsemen was to make a fast raid and get out before any superior force could arrive, if there was no superior force in the neighborhood, they might simply take over and stay. They did this so often that in time they claimed much of Europe's coastline.

The old Norse gods of war were eventually replaced by a new religion that was less bloody. In passing, however, the Vikings bequeathed their warrior instinct and their tactics to generations of European pirates. Everywhere they settled, they left their legacy.

Over time, ships of the Vikings were widely copied by the Europeans. They were also altered and enlarged, giving them more decks for cargo, men, supplies, and eventually cannon. Aloft, the single square sail of the Norse ship evolved into several sails, with more masts, all enabling ever-greater voyages of discovery and conquest. In the most seaworthy ships ever built, and with cannon and other weapons more powerful than any of their time, the maritime nations of Europe had the means to plunder the world as quickly as they could explore it.

Portuguese sailors found their way around Africa, opening the route east to India and the Spice Isles beyond (soon to be exploited by the Dutch). Spanish mariners probed west, first under Columbus, and then, as gold was found, with growing fleets. Famously, Hernando Cortez landed on Mexico's east coast in 1519 with a small handful of vessels and men. Marching into the heart of the Aztec empire with fewer than two hundred soldiers, he immediately took sides in the local wars that he found, defeating the enemies of his chosen friends, with their help.

The Aztec warriors fought primarily with war clubs and other weapons that were unable to dent the armor of the Spanish soldiers, who attacked with a thunder of musketry belching fire and smoke, and rode among them on trained war horses that could kill by kicking as their riders brought slaughter with their deadly long steel swords. The locals had never seen anything like it. The conquistadores also had the advantage of tactics and martial disciplines that soon swept away any opposition to the chosen allies of Cortez. In this way he enlarged his own forces, until at last he brought down Mexico's Aztec empire in the process of looting it. Hundreds of pounds of gold and silver jewelry was plucked of its precious gemstones, and then melted into ingots to be shipped back to Spain.

The discovery of the Pacific Ocean on the western side of Panama's narrow isthmus (joining North and South America) provided thousands of more miles of unknown continent. Under Juan Rodriguez Cabrillo, a squadron sailed north, charting the

| FROM VIKINGS TO CONQUISTADORES

coast of California, meeting natives with seagoing canoes built of planks. Under Francisco Pizarro, a land expedition went south, finding the mines of Peru that would yield not only gold but silver in the thousands of tons, plus precious gems of many kinds, riches beyond the dreams of men.

Everywhere, the conquistadores greeted the native peoples with smiles of friendship, but they wore their armor and kept their superior weapons at the ready. In exchange for what they wanted, they brought priests and a new religion to guide the natives spiritually through the loss of their pagan gods, and the loss of their wealth.

The new arrivals also brought diseases (such as smallpox and measles) that were previously unknown in the Americas. Having no immunity to the European sicknesses, whole native populations were decimated by them. This was entirely unintended by the conquistadores. After all, the aboriginal people were needed as a labor force, for the building of towns and forts, to work the mines, and to grow the food needed by a new empire. By decree of the Catholic Church in Rome, the natives could not be bought and sold like slaves, but it was agreed between the Church and the State that it was necessary to subjugate and convert them.

Having perpetrated what may be seen as the greatest act of piracy in the history of the Americas, Spain undertook to exploit, settle, and defend the continent it claimed, along with all of its seas, gulfs, bays, and multiple hundreds of islands. But claiming New Spain was easier than defending it, as things worked out. Spain was by no means the only piratical nation of that time, and its success immediately invited attack by other sea dogs with faster ships and skills that were at least equal to Spain's own.

THE SEA DOGS: LOOTING THE LOOTERS

Noting well the Spanish successes in America's warmer reaches, envious neighbors explored its colder northern coasts. In the Vikings' wake, ships went out from France, and especially England, competing for similar finds, but without similar success. There was plenty of land, and by the time Protestant Queen Elizabeth I took the throne of England in 1558, her nation's explorers had claimed huge chunks of North America. But its winters were hard; fierce, warrior-like native peoples lived there; and there was none of the silver, bullion, or gems that had so enriched Catholic Spain. Elizabeth's rival monarch, Philip II, could buy arms, armies, fleets, and great political influence, particularly in Rome, where Spanish conquests were sanctified by the Pope. But Philip could not secure the seas that had to be crossed by Spanish treasure ships in order to bring the booty safely home.

Elizabeth disputed Philip's claims, but her kingdom was small and poor by comparison, and she could not afford a war. To her advantage, however, she had an island nation – a fortress ringed with a moat of ocean – and a population of seafarers with traditions dating back to Viking times: Walter Raleigh, Richard Grenville, Martin Frobisher, John Hawkins, Thomas Cavendish, and especially Francis Drake. "My Sea Dogs," she called them, singling out Drake, whom she called "My Pyrate." All together, Elizabeth's skilled mariners were her stable of knights in the chess game of politics between nations.

SIR FRANCIS DRAKE

As a boy in Devonshire, England, Francis Drake was trained in ship handling, seamanship, and piloting by his father. He also learned navigation, using a mariner's astrolabe to measure the angle of the sun or a star to find latitude on the ocean's plane. His earliest command was part of an English convoy that was sent out to trade with the ports of New Spain. The Spaniards smilingly let the English in, and then ambushed them in an act of treachery that Drake never forgot or forgave. In Drake, Spain had made an enemy it could have done without. He escaped the ambush and the slaughter of his countrymen to limp home to England, and when he revisited New Spain, it was with a thirst for revenge. His force was small, but his tactic was to strike without warning at the places where the Spaniards had gathered their wealth. Secretly landing an armed force behind the enemy's fortifications, he would then bombard them from the front with his cannon, drawing attention, while his landing party burst in from the undefended rear.

It worked again and again, but it was a dangerous play. In the chess game between nations, Drake was a knight, and knights were sacrificial. King Philip was stung by the English pirates, and their raids soon strained diplomacy between the two nations. The sea dog's survival depended upon bringing home enough wealth to justify the political tension he was causing.

After scouring the Caribbean Sea and the Spanish main, Drake set his sights on the richest and most vulnerable prize of all – the whole undefended Pacific coast of North America. There the Spanish governors had never seen an enemy ship. The continent of America stretched south like a long wall into the most dangerous waters of the world, off Cape Horn, as its southern tip would be called. Only there could a ship pass between the oceans. Ferdinand Magellan, the great Portuguese explorer, had made the passage and gone on to circumnavigate the globe. Drake reckoned that he could do it too, and more profitably.

To that end, Drake sailed from England in 1577 with three small ships and one hundred and sixty men. Good looting was expected, and perhaps other rewards, such as a northern passage between the oceans that would be more apparent from the Pacific than the Atlantic side, where it had eluded discovery. With such a waterway, England would have all the seas at its fingertips.

Off Cape Horn, Drake's little squadron was blasted by the furious storms for which it is famous, " . . . as if all the clouds under heaven had been called together to lay their force upon one place." Of his three ships, one was swallowed by the sea, and another driven back, but Drake's *Golden Hind*

fought through. With this one small vessel he pressed north into warmer waters and fairer winds. The Spanish ports and local ships were undefended, as expected, and he fell like a thunderbolt on both. In one place, he landed and took an entire pack train of mules loaded with silver ingots; in another, he captured a galleon carrying twenty-six tons of silver, eighty pounds of gold, thirteen chests of coin, plus jewel and plate. When the English guns spoke, the treasure was theirs. *Golden Hind* was better armed and faster than any locally built craft, so she stayed ahead of any alarm, skirting the coast northward – past Peru, Panama, Mexico, and beyond – probing for a passage that might make a northern route home. Instead, Drake found only headwinds off the coast of what is today northern California, which he named Nova Albion for its resemblance to England's white cliffs.

Somewhere near today's San Francisco, he found a sheltered beach where his ship could be careened, hoisted over on her side to get her bottom burned and scraped clean of weeds and barnacles. Making friends with the local people, he resupplied the *Golden Hind* with water and provisions.

In order to return home, Drake sailed west across the uncharted Pacific and the Indian Ocean, rounding Africa on his way to England with the richest trove of loot that had ever been seen there. Rather than being arrested for piracy, Drake was knighted.

Not pleased, Philip of Spain chose war. If he could not contain England, he would invade it. In order to do that, he began to gather ships, men, and materials for a fleet that would be large and powerful enough to land an overwhelming army on the island, and simply take it.

Elizabeth soon learned of the invasion plans, and that Philip was gathering his fleet at Cadiz. Again Drake struck, with a squadron of warships making a surprise visit to that major Spanish port, sailing right into the harbor before its defenses could be raised. Inside, he sent out boats loaded with soldiers and well-armed sailors to torch all of the warehouses and shipping in sight. This they did with great efficiency, and then sailed out again as Cadiz burned.

Drake's attack delayed the onslaught of Philip's fleet, his armada, for a year. When it came at last, England was better prepared. Into the English Channel sailed the grandest fleet ever seen in those waters, bristling with men and guns in over-whelming force. Elizabeth's sea dogs were there to meet the Spanish. They were too few to break the armada's formation, but the English ships were faster and handier, and they harassed the enemy fleet around its edges. When the armada anchored off Flanders in order to pick up the Spanish army awaiting it there, Drake's idea was to send blazing fire ships into the enemy anchorage. In the confusion of trying to get out of their way, the armada was fragmented; the English ships pounded the galleons with superior gunnery, sinking or dis-abling a few, but scattering all. A shift in the wind prevented their return to the English Channel.

At last, helter-skelter, the fragmented Spanish armada was forced to sail north around the British Isles in order to return to Spain, but many vessels never made it. Off the west coast of Scotland and Ireland, they were hard hit by a series of westerly gales that drove galleon after galleon onto the rocks. Of those that survived, none would ever again trouble Drake.

Elizabeth's pirate ended his career as it had begun, campaigning against the Spaniards in the West Indies, where he was struck down by yellow fever in 1596.

— 3 —

THE ARISTOCRATIC PIRATES

hile some European pirates spread their sails to distant oceans, others carried on with business in their home waters. Ashore, there had come boundaries between nations, with rule by law, but there was no law for the sea. As in the Dark Ages, any sail on the horizon could represent danger. There were not yet standing navies to squelch the freelance pirates, and there were also "privateers" to worry about. Privateers were private warships that operated much as pirates did, but were sanctioned by authorities such as ports or governments. Also there were aristocratic landholders who considered their hereditary coasts as their own and patrolled them with vigor. Passing ships that were taxed or taken captive provided good revenue to whole communities, from the landholder on down.

Such was the situation along Ireland's wild Connaught coast, in the lands ruled by Dubhdara, chieftain of Murrisk and of the clan O'Malley, a famous seagoing clan. While most aristocratic ship owners hired professional captains to handle their squadrons, Dubhdara was a formidable sailor who commanded his own ships whenever he could break

free from his lordly responsibilities ashore. The chieftain fathered a son, who would become a bagpiper, and a daughter, who would be known to history as "the pirate queen of Ireland." The English called her Grace O'Malley, but in Gaelic Ireland she was *Granuaile* (pronounced "Gran-you-ale").

Born around 1530, Dubhdara's daughter became his pride and his chosen successor, to which end he trained her from childhood. Her first lesson in small boat handling likely happened in an Irish coracle. Later, she accompanied him on coastal trips, and then on trading passages to distant lands such as Spain, always with on-deck schooling in all the sailing arts from a skilled father commanding a crew of tough sailors. By the time Granuaile grew into young womanhood (and a handsome woman she was, a dark-haired beauty by all accounts), she had been schooled in Latin – the common language of literate Europe – as well as the arts of politics, diplomacy, and war.

The Irish clans had been feuding among themselves for centuries, but by the time of Dubhdara's death, all of western Ireland was under attack by an English army sent by Queen Elizabeth I to subjugate the place and force its clan chieftains to swear fealty to England. Many had done so, but Granuaile's response was to step up attacks on English shipping in and out of Galway instead. For that she was branded a pirate, but there was no catching her fleet of fast galleys. Similar to the Viking ships of former times, these could be rowed, or sailed, or beached for repairs under the battlements of her raiders' lair on Clare Isle in Clew Bay, well sheltered from the northwesterly gales.

At around age sixteen, Granuaile married the son of a clan allied against the English, a soldier known as "Donal of the Battles." Donal was mostly away fighting on land while his young wife attended to the ships, the administration of her territories, and the two sons and a daughter that she bore him before he was killed in battle.

Her next love was a shipwrecked, half-drowned young mariner whom she found washed ashore on Clare Isle and nursed back to health. Her happiness was short-lived, as her sailor was murdered by warring clansmen on the Isle of Doona. Granuaile led an attack, routed their stronghold, put its defenders to the sword, and added the place to her own holdings. After that, she was known as "The Dark Lady of Doona." Another of her nicknames was "Grace of the Gamblers," because she liked to gamble with the men she led in battle or at sea.

Granuaile never allowed her seafaring to be interrupted, even by pregnancy. Eventually marrying again (a war chieftain of the clan Burke called "Iron Richard," after the armor he usually wore), she became pregnant with a third son who was born at sea on a trading voyage to Spain. The following day, while she was nursing her new infant, her ship was attacked by Saracen pirates. Granuaile stayed below until, with the intruders seemingly gaining the upper hand, she charged above with a blunderbuss, yelling to her hard-pressed men, "Can't you do without me for even a day?" Shamed as Irishmen, they rallied, capturing the enemy ship.

The English were not so easily disposed of. Bit by bit Queen Elizabeth's forces nibbled away at Murrisk, until at last they captured Granuaile. She was sentenced to death and imprisoned for a year and a half, long enough to watch some of her fellow rebels hanged for crimes far less serious than piracy. So she bargained, eventually making the formal submission that secured her release. She used her freedom to rebuild her forces in order to fight on, which she did, on and on, against all odds. Granuaile grew old in the fighting. She saw her people burned from their homes, their cattle driven off, and her best fighters slaughtered or hanged. Her second husband died in battle, and one by one her sons were swallowed by English jails. At last, at age sixty-two, seeing a dark future with nothing but more blood and no gain, Granuaile was left with no choice but submission, real submission this time, in exchange for her life and whatever other favors she might be able to get from the victors. But she would handle it in her own way.

She was still as canny a bargainer as always, starting with her chosen mode of surrender. Instead of turning herself in to the dubious mercy of the English governor she had been fighting, she avoided him by putting to sea in command of one of her galleys. This she navigated south around Ireland and England, then through the Dover Straits, threading the hazards of the Thames to London, where she landed, requesting an audience with Queen Elizabeth herself. It was a brash thing to do, and it worked.

Apparently, the pirate queen of England was bemused by the notion of a chat with the pirate queen of Ireland, because she granted the interview, and the two met on good terms. In contrast to Elizabeth's bejeweled and richly costumed court, Granuaile wore her plain, fur-lined chieftain's cloak. The two powerful women were able to talk at length in Latin, the language they held in common. They must have got on very well indeed, because when they parted, Granuaile had secured the royal pardon for herself, her sons, and her people, plus an income from her family estates for the rest of her life.

Both Granuaile and Elizabeth died peacefully in their beds in the year 1603. Both are remembered as national heroines in their countries today, whatever their piratical tendencies. By no means did piracy die with them, however. Granuaile's youngest son, called "Theobold of the Ships" (he who was born at sea on the eve of battle), would famously carry on the family trade into another generation, and Elizabeth's "Sea Dogs" spawned a century of buccaneers.

4

THE BROTHERHOOD
OF THE COAST

With the advent of national navies during the 1600s, piracy was doomed in northern Europe, but the West Indies offered a happy hunting ground with very inviting opportunities. The settlements that Spain had seeded there after Columbus had ripened into a sprawling colonial empire, producing ever-increasing wealth, but the vast Spanish claims were just as impossible to defend as they had been in Drake's time. The many islands were particularly vulnerable to capture by competitive maritime powers, primarily England, France, and the Netherlands. All wanted their own pieces of the West Indies, which offered ports for repairing and supplying their ships and plenty of land for plantations worked by cheap labor. Black slaves were used for the hardest toil, and indentured Europeans for everything else needed in a colonial island society.

Although the indentured workers were not called slaves, all had signed a contract that put them in a position they couldn't get out of. The same was true for the sailors who worked the naval ships under iron discipline and brutal conditions, and the soldiers who were sent out to the tropics to defend whatever island they were assigned to, and to build its forts.

Inevitably, some slaves managed to run away; indentured workers fled their contracts; sailors jumped ship, and soldiers deserted. There were smuggling sloops needing crew, and plenty of other islands to run to. Some of these islands supported small communities of fellow refugees, independent-minded people of every color, nationality, and religion, making a very tolerant society in which skills and deeds were held to be more important than beliefs, and everybody had a say in the ruling council. From these people sprang the buccaneers, or *boucaniers*, as they were originally called in French.

THE
CARIBBEAN SEA
&
SPANISH MAIN
&
ADJACENT WATERS
1 6 9 0

NEW-
FOUND-
LAND

NOVA SCOTIA
MAHONE BAY

BOSTON
CAPE COD
NEW YORK

CAPE HATTERAS

CHARLES TOWN

BERMUDA

FLORIDA

NEW ORLEANS

ATLANTIC OCE

GULF of MEXICO

BAHAMAS
NASSAU

CUBA

MEXICO

CAYMEN ISLANDS

TORTUGA

JAMAICA
PORT ROYAL

HISPANIOLA
SANTO DOMINGO

PUERTO RICO

GUADELOUPE

SANTA CATALINA

CARIBBEAN SEA

MARTINIQUE

BARBADOS

SPANISH MAIN

PACIFIC
OCEAN

CARTAGENA
CHAGRES PORTOBELLO
PANAMA

MARACAIBO

TRINIDAD

TIERRA FIRME

GALAPAGOS ISLANDS

GUAYAQUIL

EQUATOR

W
G

Many of the islands of the West Indies swarmed with wild animals, especially pigs. When prepared properly, dried and smoked, their meat made a valuable provision that kept well in a time before refrigeration. It had a high market value to the hunter who was a good enough marksman with his long musket to bring down a running pig in the forest. By the mid-1600s, bands of such hunters had formed, most famously on the island of Tortuga, which had been claimed by the French. The islanders named the pig-hunters' product after the hut in which the strips of meat were smoked, the *boucan.* Hence, the hunters became *boucaniers.*

By all accounts, they were a rowdy lot, living in forest camps, or on a beach where turtling and fishing was good, and bringing their product to the nearest friendly port by sea. There, they could sell their goods, buy supplies, and carouse in the taverns before returning to the hunt. Their only enemies were the Spanish war parties that were randomly sent out to hunt them down and kill them. The Spaniards were famed for their cruelty, and their jealousy for what they considered their own territory, which was the entire Spanish main and all the Caribbean and beyond, including the bits claimed and held by others. All buccaneers were united by their common hatred of Spaniards, attacking them at every opportunity.

There were a lot of opportunities, particularly at sea, where the French *boucaniers* attacked Spanish shipping, as did the English buccaneers, and the Dutch and Flemish "sea beggars." All had armed vessels, and most had "letters of marque," privateers' commissions from at least one colonial governor authorizing the capture of Spanish vessels. In exchange for this privilege, a governor's privateers gave him his best defense force against any attack on his island, as well as a share of their booty. From that, and from the taxes gathered on his plantations, the governor was expected to enrich first his home government, then himself and his local administration, while expanding trade. There was good money to be made all around.

Engraved by an unknown artist, the attached copperplate portrait of a boucanier *is the only contemporary representation that has survived. It puts the pig hunter under a palm tree (with his camp in the background and his dogs at his side) holding his long* fusil boucanier – *a weapon that was named for him – and smoking his pipe. His calves are bound for protection against sharp undergrowth; he wears the simple tunic of a sailor, a cap with upturned visor, and his hunting accoutrements at his left side. These were a pouch and a short cutlass, as shown in detail on the more modern interpretation to the right, the same subject in reverse view.*

Buccaneers haunted the trade routes of the Caribbean and its adjacent waters, sometimes joining forces to land a surprise visit on a Spanish town where wealth had been gathering. The favorite tactic of the buccaneers was to appear from nowhere, strike swiftly, get what they had come for, and be gone before any larger force could get there to dispute things. It worked as well for the brotherhood as it had for Drake, and for the Vikings before that.

The buccaneers had talented commanders of their own, the most successful being those few who could draw together a squadron of fully independent ships, often under different flags, and keep them together and cooperating for the duration of a campaign. The most notable of these was known to history as Sir Henry Morgan, and to the Spaniards as "the scourge of the Indies."

Morgan was a burly Welshman who sailed to the Caribbean with the English expedition that captured Jamaica in 1655, when his talents were well enough noticed to get him command of a ship. This led to squadrons of others, which he led to the sack of such major Spanish ports as Maracaibo and Portobelo,

with astonishing rewards – for every lowly buccaneer and on up to the English governor of Jamaica, who had given Morgan his licence. With that, Morgan cast his sights on the city of Panama, perhaps the wealthiest Spanish port in the New World, and never taken.

The city's main protection was its location on the western side of the Isthmus of Panama. There the Pacific and Atlantic oceans are separated by only some seventy miles of jungle threaded by rivers and trails. Morgan's plan was to take the Spanish harbor and fort guarding the Caribbean side, then leave his ships and move a powerful force across the Isthmus, first by canoe up the river Chagres, then by trail to their destination, which would be well defended. To make the attack, Morgan gathered the largest fleet of buccaneer ships that the Caribbean would ever see, thirty-eight vessels

of every kind, carrying two thousand brethren of the coast, sailing in a pack from their mustering point in the Cayman Islands.

According to Morgan's plan, they overwhelmed the fort at Chagres, then embarked in dugout canoes, paddling upstream as other companies on foot guarded the river's banks against Spanish ambush. None came, but there were other setbacks that Morgan had not anticipated. First, the river was lower than normal, full of shoals and snags that impeded their progress until the canoes had to be abandoned. Morgan was left with no choice but to make a forced march over trails where all bridges along their path had been burned.

Worse, hunger set in. Morgan had planned for a fast approach to Panama, with every man carrying just his weapons and food for only two or three days. But after four days of hard progress, they weren't

even halfway to where they were going, and were totally out of provisions. Among their numbers were the best hunters in the world, but every edible animal within miles had been frightened into the forest by the approach of fifteen hundred hungry, bug-bitten buccaneers making their slow way forward. By the time Morgan's men reached the grasslands at the western end of their tortured march, they were too weakened by starvation to fight anybody, but there they found Spanish cattle.

According to an eyewitness, at once they "shot down every beast within range. All got busy; while some hunted, others lit fires to roast the meat. . . . The meat scarcely had time to get hot before they grabbed it and began gnawing, gore running down their cheeks."

Thus refreshed, Morgan's troops attacked the Spanish army that was drawn up outside the city, where it could deploy its superior force of infantry and cavalry together. The Spaniards were well pre-pared, outside of Panama and within, where the alarm had been drummed and cried through the streets the previous day. Outnumbered, Morgan had no advantage of surprise this time, nor any horsemen, but his pig hunters were the best marks-men anywhere. They fought in open formations, making hard targets while sharpshooting at the close-packed Spanish formations with a fire that was deadly accurate. Under it, the defenders broke and ran, and Panama belonged to the buccaneers.

The sack of the city followed, and its burning, accompanied by acts of cruelty that Morgan's best efforts could not control. In the end, it was a dark victory, one that would forever stain his name. Nor did he find anywhere near the quantity of plunder he had expected, because the word of his coming had given the Spaniards plenty of time to hide or evacuate their wealth. Even so, during a month of

S.r HEN: MORGAN
Part.2. Chap. 4. pa79.

scavenging the invaders gathered enough silver and
other treasure to load a pack train of one hundred
and seventy-five mules for the march back to Chagres
and the fleet.

Returning to Jamaica and its infamous pirate
capital of Port Royal, Morgan was hailed by just
about everybody, especially the taverners, brothel
owners, prostitutes, and all others who had bene-
fited from the wealth that was being spread around
without having had to face cannonballs. Less
pleased were some of Morgan's captains and crews,
who felt as though the ordeals of the Panama campaign had outweighed the profits. In any case, no
buccaneering expedition of that size would ever be
mounted again.

In the end, Morgan was appointed deputy governor of Jamaica, a respectable post that he kept
until 1687, when he died from "drinking and sitting
up late," according to his physician's report.

hy did the Spanish, who knew too well the power of a swarm of privateers, have none of their own? It appears that their own warships were too busy trying to guard their treasure fleets. Also, they had little luck in recruiting foreign privateers to raid the enemies who were regularly raiding them. There was one noteworthy exception, and that was a Portuguese captain named Manoel Rivero Pardal. Rivero is remembered as a very strange man whose ambitions far outstretched his talents, both in war and in poetry.

Some of the poetry he was fond of writing has survived, and it is in celebration of himself and his deeds. One of his verses describes his sailing "the wave-filled and surging sea up to the Cayman Islands where with fire I made havoc . . . and the mob all trembled at my name." This describes his landing at a defenseless town on the British-held Cayman Islands, where he burned some fishermen's huts, to nobody's benefit, certainly not his crew's. It is said that he mustered his crew in order to read his poetical efforts to them. Their opinions are not recorded.

Rivero did manage to capture a small English vessel with eighteen men, but only with great difficulty. "I came as a punishment for the heretics," he pronounced, then sailed for Jamaica, where he made some more landings at undefended places, burning some more shacks, at last earning the irritation of the island's governor. So inspired was Rivero by his own deeds, he wrote a challenge to Morgan to come out and fight with him.

Morgan didn't, but one of his captains did, and that was the end of Rivero's ship, which was captained in the fight, and the poet himself, who was shot through the neck. He is remembered mostly because the small damage he caused gave the English governor at Port Royal the justification he needed to authorize a reprisal, which was Morgan's devasting attack on Panama.

5

TO THE INDIAN OCEAN

hat with all of the privateers, buccaneers, "sea beggars," corsairs, mahons, filibusters, and unlicensed out-and-out renegades fishing the West Indies year after year, its waters were overworked. At the same time, the tastiest prey, the Spaniards, had stiffened their defenses, both ashore and at sea, where Spain's treasure galleons were better protected by ever more warships firing ever more cannonballs.

By the late 1600s, some of the more adventurous English buccaneers had found better fishing in the Indian Ocean. It was a longer, more grueling voyage than to the Caribbean, but worth it if you could get there. The ships of the Moghul Empire of India carried wealth rivaling Spain's, as did Arabian dhows, in and out of the Red Sea and the Persian Gulf. None of these was a match for the superior warships of the western pirates. The Indian Ocean became the new ocean of no rules. The European nations had all staked out their trading posts there, to be sure, and any unlicensed attack on, for instance, a ship flying the colors of the British East India Company could lead to consequences. But snapping up a "heathen" ship was not so risky, and there were lots of them.

When Captain Thomas Tew returned from the Indian Ocean to his native New England colony of Rhode Island in 1694, his cargo was gold, gemstones and jewelry, silver, brocades, silken fabrics, ivory, and other treasure that paid every common sailor in his crew some three thousand pounds sterling, enough to support anyone for the rest of his life in great comfort. Being sailors, most of them spent it quickly, to the great joy of the local economy.

Tew became an instant celebrity, toasted by all and courted by the best society. This included

Rhode Island's royal governor, who gladly wrote him a licence to make another cruise and do it all again. Tew had no trouble in raising another crew, with "servants from most places of the country running from their masters, sons from their parents," all zealous to sign aboard for his next adventure. And he returned with more treasure, inspiring more imitators, who were quickly approved by the crown governors of New England. Tew's luck was cut short by a cannonball through his stomach on his next voyage, but by then the Indian Ocean was on the "pirate's round," with plenty of competition, but lots of loot for all.

The infamous Henry Avery took another astoundingly rich prize in 1695. This was a ship belonging to no less than the Great Moghul of the Indian Empire, carrying not just his wealth but his friends and family as well. After overwhelming a bloody but futile defense, the buccaneers swarmed over the rail of the Moghul ship with a ferocity that turned into cruel slaughter. Some of the women passengers wound turbans around their heads to make them look like boys, and hid their children as best they could, but none was spared. Among all the pirate atrocities of history, Avery's is one of the most memorable. It certainly did not improve the Moghul's feeling toward Englishmen, and his reaction was to retaliate against the British East India Company (suspecting collusion between it and the pirates) by refusing to do business with one of England's most valuable trading arms.

Into this atmosphere sailed a Scottish-born captain, William Kidd, a successful buccaneer veteran of the Caribbean. Kidd had married well in New York and settled there peacefully, with three children and a family church pew, until he was inspired to follow Tew and Avery to the Indian Ocean. For the adventure that was going to make him notorious in the annals of piracy, he journeyed to England, where he obtained a thirty-gun ship, *Adventure Galley*, with the backing of aristocratic and wealthy patrons in London who would share in the expected profits. Kidd's licence authorized his attack only on pirates (such as Tew) and ships flying the colors of France (with whom England was at war), but it was well understood by all that the ocean of no rules would yield other treasures. Kidd had no trouble fleshing out his crew in New York before proceeding around Africa in time to pick up the seasonal monsoon that would carry him into the Indian Ocean.

Kidd found his great prize there, but only after a torturous, year-long voyage that wore out his ship and demoralized his crew. In an argument with the ship's gunner, whom Kidd had deemed mutinous, he whacked the man on his head with a bucket, killing him. The mood on board improved only with the capture of some small prizes, plus one big one, a five-hundred-ton dhow bearing more than enough treasure to justify everything *Adventure Galley* had gone through.

There remained only the need to get back to New England, after a necessary stop at Isle Sainte Marie, Madagascar, where, a harbor of refuge and a base for buccaneers working the pirate's round was conveniently placed. A regular trade had been established there by some canny New York merchants who became rich by providing all the necessary supplies that were unavailable so far from home: shoes, shirts, nails, gunpowder, marline, tobacco, muskets and cannon, Malagasy girls, *boucan*, and rum by the bottle or the keg. All could be had in exchange for diamonds, fabrics, ivory, and gold.

The establishment was enclosed by a palisade to protect its cattle and slave pens, also the factor's house and the tavern and store offering every amusement sea-weary sailors could want. At the time of

46   TO THE INDIAN OCEAN

Kidd's visit in 1698, the New York factor at Isle Sainte Marie was Edward Welch, who profited greatly from Kidd's success.

So did the governor of New York when Kidd returned there with the take, although not in the way Kidd had expected. Instead of toasting his success, the governor (who was one of the voyage's investors) arrested Kidd and confiscated his treasure trove. Too late, Kidd learned that the system had changed during his long voyage. At last, the murderous depredations of the western pirates had left behind enough angry "heathens" to damage Britain's valuable, legitimate trade with India. Kidd found himself the target of their wrath and British blame. Instead of backing him for having made a good job of his assignment, his influential patrons abandoned him, and he was shipped to London in irons to await trial. It was to be a two-year wait. As the politics of his case played out in comfortable drawing rooms, Kidd remained chained in a stone cell among the stink and vermin of London's Newgate prison, hoping for a pardon.

It never came. Too many powerful Englishmen were embarrassed by their involvement in piracy all the way up to the monarchy itself. Also, there was the Moghul to be placated, with East India Company profits at stake. Kidd's only remaining value was as the sole scapegoat for the mess, and the result of his trial was a foregone conclusion. Two hours before the proceedings began, Kidd was given a lawyer, but not the documents he needed to mount a defense (they had mysteriously vanished). Nor was the defendant allowed to call witnesses, although many were called against him.

Following his conviction (first for murdering his gunner with a water bucket, and after that for piracy), his hanging was scheduled for two weeks later, which gave his jailers plenty of chance to make some money from all who were willing to pay for a look at the condemned celebrity. Many came, and on the spring day of Kidd's execution in 1701, much of London turned out to watch him paraded in a cart, which stopped now and again so that he could be handed drinks along the way. Under the gallows he was allowed to proclaim to the mob some of the things he'd been unable to get into his trial, ending with his advice to sailors to be cautious and prudent. Then there was a psalm and a prayer, and a drop. Kidd's rope broke, so he got two drops, and the second one did the trick.

At last, there was only one more use for Kidd, which was his body's display at Tilbury Point on the Thames. There, all mariners passing in or out of London could view his shriveling corpse, held together by chains and iron hoops, a silent testament to his own last advice to fellow sailors toward prudence and caution.

As to the booty that Kidd had brought back, and which had been confiscated from him, none of it ever found its way back to the people from whom it had been stolen.

fter Kidd, England tried to suppress piracy in the Indian Ocean whenever possible, but its myriad islands were entirely too vast to patrol. The frigates of the Royal Navy and the East India Company were tasked with the destruction of pirates in those waters; there were to be hot encounters between them for many years thereafter, not always to the advantage of the government ships.

On a summer day in 1720, among the Seychelle Islands north of Madagascar, Captain Macrea of the Royal East India Company ship *Cassandra* was pounced upon by two well-known English pirates, John Taylor and Edward England, together greatly outgunning his own ship. In a slow but deadly battle fought in a very light breeze, *Cassandra* was badly shot up but held her own. When one of the pirate vessels put out banks of oars and tried to approach *Cassandra* by rowing, Macrea shot away her oars with grapeshot.

In the end, he lost his ship, but not his life. Because of the respect he had earned from the pirate Edward England for his stalwart defense, Macrea was given one of the smaller pirate vessels that he had shot up during the action, along with a native crew, and sent safely on his way.

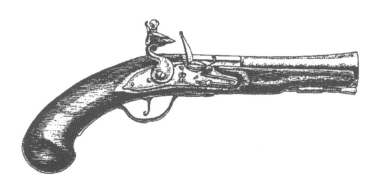

6

WOODES ROGERS: FROM PRIVATEER TO PIRATE CATCHER

hen the foreign trade of the European nations was threatened by freelance privateers, authorities made every effort to repress them – except for their own, of course, which were still licensed to attack the shipping of warring countries. The rules had stiffened, but wars continued, and there were still opportunities for a talented corsair. None was more talented than Captain Woodes Rogers, whose opportunity came in 1708 during Queen Anne's War, the latest skirmish in England's ongoing argument with Spain.

At twenty-nine, Rogers was a well-credentialed captain. One observer described him as "a man who walks with great determination." His design was to follow Drake's stormy path around Cape Horn and then north along Spanish America's Pacific coast, which was, by all reports, as badly defended as ever. Like Drake, Rogers intended to make surprise shore raids along the way, but when he reached Cape St. Lucas at the southern tip of Mexico's Baja Peninsula, he expected to take the

juiciest prize sailing the Western Ocean, the plum of plums, the annual "Manila galleon."

That treasure ship contained a cargo as precious as any known, the annual wealth the Spaniards had gathered to send home from their Oriental empire, all packed into the biggest ship available. Departing from the Philippines, then touching at Guam, the great ship's course was east with the annual trade winds that would carry her across the Pacific to California. There, she would follow the coast southward, passing Cape St. Lucas on her way to Acapulco, where the cargo would be taken by land to the Caribbean coast and shipped in a well-protected convoy to Spain. It was a long voyage, but the safest, barring an unforeseen event – which is exactly what Woodes Rogers planned to be.

To that purpose, a group of wealthy Bristol investors gave Rogers command of two frigates, *Duke*, with twenty-eight guns, and *Duchess*, with twenty-six, together carrying three hundred and thirty-three men. It was a small but powerful force, well suited to its piratical mission. Although Rogers's privateer documents saved him from being branded a buccaneer, he did enlist a few, most notably William Dampier as pilot. Dampier was not only a veteran captain of buccaneers, he was a famed navigator and cartographer – a valuable asset in the barely charted seas where Rogers planned to sail.

Crossing the Atlantic, Rogers suppressed a budding mutiny, then rounded Cape Horn, making his first Pacific stop at Juan Fernandez Island for fresh water and provisions. In a vast ocean, Juan Fernandez was a dot, isolated and uninhabited. As it happened, it did have one surprise resident when Rogers arrived, a Scottish sailing master named

Alexander Selkirk who had been marooned there some four and a half years earlier by the previous buccaneer squadron to pass that way. Having been left with a musket, kettle, and the basic tools for survival, Selkirk had survived very well indeed. His island was a seven-by-twelve-mile tip of an extinct volcano, full of craggy peaks with lush valleys, springs, caves, and a temperate climate with abundant vegetation. Varieties of vegetables and fruits grew wild; its shallows offered shellfish, lobster, and turtles; and the hills swarmed with wild goats.

When Selkirk began to run out of gunpowder, he explored the island's maze of goat trails and learned to catch the nimble animals by outrunning them. He skinned and ate quite a lot of goats while there – over five hundred by the tally that he carefully kept. Digestive problems were cured by peppercorns that produced good "wind." When he was troubled by rats, he made friends with some of the island's feral cats, and in time, after freeing his mind from the anguish of hopelessly watching for a sail on the horizon, he settled more comfortably into his accidental kingdom. Later, Selkirk would recall his solitary years on Juan Fernandez as the best in his life.

When Rogers found him there, it was hard to tell who was the more astonished, the commodore or the castaway. Selkirk could barely speak – not entirely from surprise, mostly because he had forgotten how. By Rogers's account, he looked more wild than the goats whose skins he wore. To the crew, he was immediately known as "the Governor." With the help of his local knowledge, *Duke* and *Duchess* were quickly reprovisioned and on their way, with a cleaned-up Selkirk appointed by Rogers to his former rank of sailing master.

Rogers pressed north, capturing several small prizes and pausing only long enough to raid the town of Guayaquil, which yielded a satisfactory take in treasure, goods, and hostages for ransom. Under the iron discipline of Rogers's command, there was none of the rape or horror that Morgan's men had visited on Panama.

When the Manila galleon appeared off Cape St. Lucas in December 1709, Rogers was on station there, awaiting it. The action was brief. The galleon took heavy fire from both of the English ships, particularly *Duke*, which Rogers maneuvered into a position ahead of her. From there he could blast the Spaniards with raking fire, "so warmly that she soon struck her colours . . ."

The English took few casualties, but Rogers was one of them. In his words: "I was shot through the left cheek, the bullet struck away a great part of my upper jaw and several of my teeth, part of which dropped down upon the deck." And two days later: "In the night I felt something clog my throat, which I swallowed with much pain, and suppose it is a part of my jawbone." Prevented by his wound from talking, he issued his orders in writing during a second action. There were *two* Manila galleons that year, as they learned from their prisoners.

The second galleon was even richer than the first. She was also much tougher and larger, so massive that her thick sides deflected the English six-pounder cannonballs, whereas her heavier guns were able to punish the attackers at will, repelling any attempt to board with small arms, grenades, and firebombs. Rogers was wounded again, this time by a big splinter striking him in the left foot, "part of my heel bone being struck out and all my ankle cut above half through." His crew were faring no better. With no chance of taking the huge ship, just more casualties, he withdrew to lick his wounds. There had been a heavy butcher's bill all around, although Selkirk didn't take a scratch.

After the action, and in his terrible condition, Rogers managed to deflect another mutiny, and to repair and provision his ships on that remote coast. Then he crossed the Pacific and the Indian oceans, rounding Africa for the northward haul back to England, completing his circumnavigation of the world. He had sailed some forty-five thousand miles, accomplishing every detail of his mission while keeping his ships together the whole way.

Rogers also brought home handsome profits to all involved, including Selkirk, whose share worked out to eight hundred pounds, a very great deal of money at that time. It could be said that Alexander

Selkirk's story was the longest-lived part of all the treasure that Rogers brought back, because it inspired Daniel Defoe's *Robinson Crusoe,* which was that author's embellished version of Selkirk's tale. In Robert Louis Stevenson's *Treasure Island,* Selkirk inspired the marooned Ben Gunn; in *Swiss Family Robinson* he became an entire family.

As for Rogers, the conclusion of Queen Anne's War in 1713 started a chain of events that pitted him against the entire brotherhood of the coast. The last generation of buccaneers and privateers were all thrown out of work with the unwelcome Treaty of Utrecht, which declared total peace among the warring nations of Europe for the first time in living memory. This left quite a lot of unemployed but well-armed buccaneers with no more bases, but scores of efficient warships with nobody to fight, and no other way of making a living. It was a recipe for pirate stew, and the brotherhood made a base at Nassau on Providence Island in the Bahamas.

The Bahamas had been settled by England, but had been abandoned by its governor after repeated attacks during the war, leaving the place up for grabs. The buccaneers grabbed it, and by 1717 it was a thriving refuge for all kinds of unsupervised activities, some more legal than others. Hunting, fishing, turtling, and cutting logwood provided a living, as did diving on some wrecks of Spanish treasure ships, sunk in a hurricane in 1715, until the Spaniards showed up in force and took over the salvage. Better was smuggling, always an option in the West Indies, and, most profitably, continued raids on Spanish shipping, treaties be damned.

Nassau was only a ramshackle collection of structures, mostly roofed with sails, but it had a good harbor guarded by a fort with an eighteen-pounder cannon, and the place made an ideal nest for many enterprises. England was alarmed enough to appoint Woodes Rogers as governor general of the Bahamas, with the task of taking over the place and cleaning it up.

7

ON THE ACCOUNT

Woodes Rogers's appointment as captain general and governor in chief of the entire Bahamian archipelago gave him vast authority, but nowhere near enough warships (two) or men (a hundred soldiers) to take the place away from the thousand or so buccaneers who had taken root and refuge there. Not if they chose to resist.

Nor would Rogers have the advantage of surprise. Months before his planned arrival to take up his post at Nassau, a proclamation had been dispatched there announcing his advent, and that he would come with the king's pardon for all who were willing to give up their wicked ways.

The brotherhood's response at Nassau was to seize the ship bearing the message, and to convene a council that brought in the biggest family gathering of brethren since Morgan's time. Their sloops and schooners sailed in from the Mexican Gulf to Newfoundland. The big question for all was whether to resist or take the pardon. A fight would mean a declaration of independence from England and its empire, with inevitable and untold consequences. It was very tempting to accept, instead, a royal pardon that would forgive everything one had done, as long as one didn't do it again. In the end, that was the decision made by the majority, and Rogers's arrival was unopposed, except for one last, impudent broadside from some of those who chose to escape and carry on with their ways.

To Rogers's relief, when he stepped ashore, he was saluted by several hundred scruffy but loyal subjects, and from them he immediately began forming a militia to enforce and protect his new government. He also commissioned some of his ex-buccaneers to go out and capture their unrepentant former friends for trial and hanging, which they did.

Rogers had won by dividing the English buccaneer community between those who didn't want to declare war on their own flag, and those whose war was with the entire abusive (to poor sailors) system of the maritime world – flags and letters of marque be damned. These sailed "on the account," as it was called, meaning on their own account, a state of affairs described most eloquently by Captain Sam Bellamy.

Working the New England coast in his thirty-gun, oared frigate *Whydah Gally*, Bellamy came across a sloop in the middle of a dense fog. The master of the sloop, seeing a warship appear out of the mist, hailed it through his speaking trumpet: "Where are you from?"

"The seas," answered Bellamy, promptly seizing the sloop. Customarily, the buccaneers tried to enlist any of their prisoners who wanted to be as free as themselves. As Bellamy put it to the sloop's master when he turned down the invitation:

Damn ye, you are a sneaking puppy, and so are all those who will submit to be governed by laws which rich men have made for their own security, for the cowardly whelps have not the courage otherwise to defend what they get by their knavery. But damn ye all together. Damn them for a pack of crafty rascals, and you, who serve them, for a parcel of hen-hearted numbskulls. They vilify us, the scoundrels do, when there is only one difference, they rob under the cover of law, forsooth, and we plunder the rich under the protection of our own courage.

All of Bellamy's captives were let go safe and sound, and off sailed *Whydah* back into the mists.

Like others of the brethren, Bellamy used the outports of northeastern America, from Maine to Nova Scotia and Newfoundland, to recruit willing hands. As well, they could tuck in to a remote cove for refitting, rest, recreation, and music. Musicians were much prized, and were given an increased share of the spoils. Bellamy even staged theatrical

dramas on his quarterdeck. His luck ran out off Cape Cod, where his ship drove aground in a gale, drowning him and all of his crew except for eight, who survived the wreck to be tried and hanged in Boston. Silver pieces of eight from *Whydah*'s treasure still wash ashore off Cape Cod.

With no more major ports of refuge willing to take them, the freelance brethren still operating had to make a choice between sailing big, full-rigged ships, like *Whydah*, or smaller vessels, such as sloops. Besides firepower, the advantage of a big ship was its better ability to make long voyages. Its drawbacks included some disadvantage in chasing smaller craft, particularly in shoal waters, where a big corsair could be outmaneuvered by a clever smaller quarry. Also, with no adequate ports available for supply and repair, a big ship had to be replaced eventually by some fresher prize taken at sea.

In the Americas, the brotherhood largely got rid of bigger warships, with their bigger problems, adopting in their place the smaller, more versatile single-masted sloops used by the Bermudians and Bahamians. These could not be heavily enough gunned to fight the Royal Navy's ships, but their swivel cannon, light carriage guns, and big crews were more than a match for the average merchant vessel.

erhaps Nassau's most infamous pirate of all was William Teach, or Blackbeard, as he is known to history. He sailed for a while with a forty-gun ship named *Queen Anne's Revenge*, but abandoned her (and her crew) in favor of a ten-gun sloop, which he then used as a private, armed yacht, cruising the Carolina coasts and raiding east to Bermuda.

Teach was a big man, and a formidable competitor, worthy of his legend, but his main talent was getting what he wanted by invoking terror rather than fighting. By a contemporary account:

Captain Teach assumed the cognomen of Blackbeard from that large quantity of hair, which, like a frightful meteor, covered his whole face and frightened America more than any comet that had appeared there a long time. This beard was black, which he suffered to grow of an extravagant length. . . . He was accustomed to twist it with ribbons, in small tails. . . . In time of action he wore a sling over his shoulders with three brace of pistols and stuck lighted matches under his hat, which . . . his eyes naturally looking fierce and wild, made him altogether an idea of a fury, from hell.

Blackbeard's terror tactics worked very well . . . until, abruptly, they didn't. In 1718, two sloops under the command of a Royal Navy officer found Blackbeard at Ocracoke Inlet, off the Carolina coast, and put an end to his career in a hard-fought action. It ended with his severed head hung at the tip of his enemy's bowsprit, giving rise to the local legend of Blackbeard's ghost haunting Ocracoke Inlet, forever looking for his missing head.

Meanwhile, other Nassau refugees carved their names in history just as notoriously as Blackbeard, notably the pirates Anne Bonny and Mary Read, two women in their twenties who both dressed and posed as men, when it suited their purpose, as it did when they coincidentally signed on as crew aboard Calico Jack Rackham's sloop. There they met. Anne Bonny had abandoned a wastrel husband in order to sail away with Calico Jack. Mary Read, retired from a career in the British army, was now involved in an entirely different adventure. Both women would play the role of fierce young men when they wished, or become

desirable females by changing clothes and attitudes. By all accounts, they could both be very seductive, but dangerous. When Mary Read set her eyes on a young lover, and that individual was challenged to a duel by another buccaneer, she would take on the challenger first, with pistols and cutlasses, and blow away that threat to her chosen mate.

In 1720, Rackham's sloop was captured at Jamaica. Its whole company was put on trial, and most were given the death sentence, including Calico Jack and his two female crew. His women had been their sloop's only real defense during the brief action, fighting on after

Rackham and the men of his crew had fled below decks. There they had escaped the hail of fire from the pirate-hunting sloop that had overwhelmed them, but not their fate.

"If you had fought like a man, you wouldn't have to be hanged like a dog," Anne Bonny told Calico Jack when they were allowed to see one another before his hanging. Her own hanging was postponed because she was discovered to be pregnant at the time, which was Mary Read's condition also. Mary died in prison with a fever. Anne's fate is lost to history, except for the fact that she did not hang.

What did Anne Bonny and Mary Read actually look like? Many portraits were made of them after their popular stories were published, but their artists never saw their subjects, making for imaginative results. For instance, the 1724 engraving above shows a brutish pair with rhino-like bodies. Yet both young women were noted in contemporary accounts as very attractive when they wanted to be. A newer and opposite interpretation imagines them at ease and undisguised, having a chat on their sloop's foredeck under a sunny Caribbean sky.

8

TWILIGHT OF THE BROTHERHOOD

With the loss of their main bases, and rules ever tightening, the brotherhood's days were numbered. They were not quite finished, however, and the last of piracy's "golden era," as historians have called it, provided some of its most memorable characters. At the top of that list was Captain Bartholomew Roberts, a legitimate English mariner until 1719, when his ship was captured by the buccaneer Howel Davis. Roberts joined his captors, and showed so much talent for his new life that he got his own ship within a few weeks. It was the first of many, and the beginning of an astonishing career.

Roberts captured over two hundred vessels in little more than two years, sailing from Africa's Guinea coast to Brazil, from there to the Caribbean, then to Newfoundland, to the islands again, and back to Africa. His method was to find the best vessel for his purpose of the moment – a large ship for a long voyage, a sloop for local raiding – and to disguise it in order to approach his quarry without arousing suspicion. More than once he sailed into anchorages full of unsuspecting ships and captured them all.

While his considerable skills in seamanship and tactics distinguished Roberts among his fellow buccaneer captains, his unorthodox personal habits were near legendary. For one thing, he drank no rum, wine, or anything alcoholic; officers and crew guzzled away, but he drank only tea, which was unheard of in that company. He allowed no gambling, no women, and he dressed up for battle in finery that

included a crimson waistcoat trimmed with gold, a red-plumed hat, and a gold chain with a large diamond cross around his neck. Roberts was a very religious Christian, and he conducted daily prayer meetings that his crew was urged to attend, as well as full services on the Sabbath, with hymns.

Aside from these quarterdeck quirks, his various ships still sailed under the customary rules and laws of the brotherhood, to which all hands were required to take an oath. Each man had a vote in council, and a say in it; all plunder was shared, as spelled out, with marooning being the penalty for withholding loot; weapons were kept clean and fit for service; any personal quarrels were taken ashore, and no fights were allowed aboard the ship; there was payment for loss of a limb in action; no desertion allowed, on penalty of death. Under Roberts's command, the ship's musicians got Sundays off.

When it came to the treatment of captives, however, there were no rules. Common sailors were generally well treated. They might be questioned about the humanity of their officers, for those who had earned the hatred of their crew were most often twentieth-century notion, a romantic fiction.)

TWILIGHT OF THE BROTHERHOOD

It is true that great cruelties dominate the annals of piracy, for the horror they conjure, but the actual situation was quite often a bloodless seagoing robbery. Many prizes were just let go, along with everything they had that their captors didn't need. Some prizes were found to be needier than their captors, and were given supplies and sent on their way with a salute, sailors to sailors.

Well-heeled captives could expect more whimsical treatment, largely depending on how they impressed their captors, who sometimes tested them in playful ways. In one case, the wigs of some aristocratic gentlemen were taken from them and worn by their taker in a pile on his head as he toasted the devil. Another time, the prisoners suffered only humiliation when they were spanked by the flats of the pirates' cutlasses. One captive, Parson Boyle, was treated gently but had to suffer through readings from his own prayer book by a disrespectful buccaneer who had taken strong drink.

As to the brotherhood's law among themselves, there is no better example of pirate justice than Harry Glasby's trial. Glasby and two others had tried to desert Roberts's ship. They were captured and brought back for trial. The penalty for desertion was death. In words set down in 1724, as recorded in Captain Charles Johnson's authoritative *History of the Most Notorious Pirates:*

> All the prisoners pleaded for arrest of judgment very movingly; but the Court had such an abhorrence of their crime that they could not be prevailed upon to show mercy, till one of the judges, whose name was Valentine Ashplant, stood up and taking his pipe out of his mouth said he had something to offer to the Court on behalf of one of the prisoners; and spoke to this effect: "By God, Glasby shall not die; damn me if he shall." After this learned speech he sat down in his place and resumed his pipe. This motion was loudly opposed by all the rest of the judges. . . . But Ashplant, who was resolute in his opinion, made another pathetical speech in the following manner, "God damn ye, gentlemen. I am as good a man as the rest of you; damn my soul if ever I turned my back to any man in my life, or ever will, by God; Glasby is an honest fellow . . . and I love him. I hope he'll live and repent of what he has done; but damn me, if he must die I will die along with him." And thereupon he pulled out a pair of pistols, and presented them to some of the learned judges upon the bench, who, perceiving his argument so well supported, thought it reasonable that Glasby should be acquitted. And so they came over to his opinion and allowed it to be law.

Glasby survived, but the brotherhood did not, not as a family. Roberts's career was cut short by a cannonball in 1722, and within a decade the last of the original brethren were gone. Their methods, however, lived on, wherever freelance sea robbers and governments found them useful.

A PIRATICAL LEGACY

hen the brotherhood of the coast passed into history, so did its democratic system – a democracy created by a family of refugee sailors in open rebellion against an oppressive society. The same spirit wouldn't emerge again for another half-century. When it did, the result was the American Revolution. At that time, anyone taking up arms was called a treasonous rebel by the British government. Those with warships were branded as pirates – a label they would certainly have kept had the war not gone their way.

"**P**aul Jones the Pirate" was how John Paul Jones was known in the English press. He was by no means the only revolutionary sea hawk to carry the title of pirate, but he is by far the best remembered. To the French he was a privateer. To the Americans of his adopted land he was and is a great naval hero, called by many the father of the American Navy.

Christened John Paul in 1747 near Kirkcudbright on Scotland's maritime southwest coast, he was the son of a gardener, but was apprenticed to the sea with a merchantman when he was thirteen years old. He was small, but competitive, and very bright, earning his first command at age twenty. From there he rapidly advanced to ever better ships – but his promising career was cut short in Tobago, where he found himself facing a mutinous crew. Attacked on his quarterdeck by the ringleader, a local man, Captain Paul defended himself with his sword, running the mutineer through.

Rather than face a hostile local court with only the rest of the mutineers as witnesses, he put his ship in the hands of its agent, fled the jurisdiction, and landed in Virginia just as the Revolutionary War was about to start.

To avoid any possible murder charge catching up with him from the Caribbean, he added "Jones" to his name. Soon after, he signed aboard the first revolutionary warship to become available to him, and started the career that was to make his name famous. Pirate or not, Jones had all the instincts of one from the first, plus an ingrained understanding of their tactics.

His ship was a ten-gun sloop, fast and handy. *Providence* carried seventy men and had the same size and rig preferred by the last of the buccaneers. In her, Jones raided British shipping along the pirates' path, from Bermuda to Nova Scotia, taking sixteen prizes while artfully evading the frigates of the Royal Navy. His obvious talent was rewarded with a larger ship and a small squadron, of which he again made good use. A more adventurous mission and a proper, brand-new, twenty-gun warship, *Ranger*, was his reward.

Jones's sights were set on raiding Britannia in her home waters. France was on the brink of another war with England, and happy to provide him with stores and a base. The rebel American ambassador in Paris, Benjamin Franklin, at once noticed the peppery Jones's talents and introduced him throughout the gilded corridors of the French aristocracy – fancy treatment for a pirate!

Jones wasted no time in living up to Franklin's expectations. He was soon back at sea, this time raiding not only England's shipping but her mainland as well. By moonlight he led two boats in an attack on Whitehaven Harbor, captured its fort, stood off the townsfolk, burned as many ships as he could, and cleared out before dawn. His crew got little rest. Before noon, *Ranger* had reached Kirkcudbright Bay, where Jones had learned to sail as a boy. His next target was the mansion of the earl of Selkirk, for whom his father had worked as a gardener.

Jones had nothing personal against the earl; his notion was to carry him off as a hostage, giving Franklin something to exchange for hundreds of American sailors in English prisons. Jones's crew was more interested in loot. Landing in boats at St. Mary's Isle, Jones's piratical shore party quickly and bloodlessly captured the Selkirk mansion with no resistance. Disappointingly, the earl was away on a trip, but plenty of his valuable silverware was around. Jones had a grander idea of treasure, and he was squeamish about letting his men bag up and carry off the silver, but he would have had a mutiny on his hands if he hadn't.

The following morning, less than a day later, he got the chance to work out his nobler aims on the Royal Navy's HMS *Drake*, a twenty-gun cruiser that he handily captured in a brief but fierce action. With his prize in tow, he sailed back to France.

The damage Jones had inflicted was modest, but the effect was huge. England's mainland had suffered no invasion in hundreds of years, and the alarm spread. Throughout the British Isles, militias were mustered, fortifications were hastily repaired, and the Royal Navy went on high alert as shipping insurance rates shot skyward. As the First Lord of the Admiralty put it to his captains: "For God's sake, get to Sea instantly. . . . If you can take Paul Jones, you will be as high in the estimation of the public as if you had beat the Combined fleets."

Delighted by Jones's tweak of the British lion's tail, the French rewarded him with the heaviest ship of his career, an ex East Indiaman, which he mounted with forty guns and named *BonHomme Richard* in honor of Benjamin Franklin, after Franklin's popular pen name. Jones also got command of an entire squadron of French privateers, along with every encouragement to keep doing what he was so good at.

Jones's next plan was for a cruise around the British Isles, by way of Ireland's west coast, then

Scotland, and south again to Leith, where he intended to capture that major port, making a distraction from a planned massive invasion of England's south coast by the full military might of France. The long-brewing war between those nations was about to explode, with the Pirate Paul Jones playing a pivotal role.

Sailing north as planned, the squadron snatched up several good prizes, but it was difficult to hold together, as Jones, the renegade Scots-American, soon discovered. Trying to keep control over a swarm of independent-minded French captains was beyond even his talents. He did keep enough fragments of his squadron together for the attack on Leith, but was frustrated by a change of wind (which was just as well, because the grand invasion to the south had not happened). With guns at the ready, but surprise lost, Jones carried on southward, where he met a British merchant convoy protected by two Royal Navy ships. Night was coming on. He attacked at once, leaving the lesser of the two enemy ships to his French consorts while taking on the most powerful one in what was to be the bloodiest naval action of the war.

HMS *Serapis* was a new forty-four-gun ship that both outgunned and outsailed *BonHomme Richard* and soon began to get the upper hand. Hoping to cripple his opponent's sailing abilities, Jones directed his fire at the sails and rigging of *Serapis,* while that ship blasted away at *Richard*'s hull, smashing her cruelly. When the pair drifted together (neutralizing his enemy's sailing superiority), Jones grappled, and tried to swarm *Serapis* with boarders, but they were driven back, and a terrible standoff developed. Aloft, *Richard*'s fighting tops were well manned with sharpshooters and swivel cannon, all pouring murderous fire down onto the Englishman's exposed deck areas until her defenders were driven under the protection of her gun decks. There, the English cannon continued to destroy *Richard,* blasting her main deck battery relentlessly and blowing huge holes through her sides. The English captain, Pearson, was unable to get out of the deadly embrace, and concentrated on sinking *Richard.* When that began to look inevitable, Pearson hailed Jones, inviting his surrender, to which Jones famously replied, "I have not yet begun to fight" (or something like that), and the long, grim battle went on. At some point, one of Jones's other ships, having inexplicably stayed out of the action, sailed across *Richard*'s bows and fired a broadside, not at *Serapis*, but directly into *Richard*. In the end, the agonizing battle was concluded by one of Jones's men, who crawled out along *Richard*'s main yard to a point where he could lob a grenade down through the English main hatch. When it exploded, it touched off a flash fire that devastated the English crew, and Pearson surrendered. It was a lucky thing for Jones, because his ship was sinking. Transferring his crew to *Serapis*, he limped across the North Sea into Dutch waters, safety, and immortality.

To France's grand scheme to invade England, Jones brought the sole success. Soirees were held in his honor, and presentations; medals were made, paintings painted, and a bust was chiseled in marble by Houdin, sculptor to the court of Louis XIV, a rare honor for a pirate.

Today, Jones's remains are entombed in marble in the chapel of the United States Naval Academy, far removed from the shadow of any gallows.

PIRATES THEN TO NOW

Going into the 1800s, the great age of sail entered its last century, and the seas and oceans of the world were still swept by pirates of various sorts. To the east, native pirate craft swarmed all trade routes from the Gulf of Aden through the South China Sea, where great fleets of them were sometimes more powerful than the rulers of the land. Western merchantmen sailing there were sure to go heavily armed.

Nor had the western sea powers altogether stamped out piracy closer to home. In the busy Mediterranean, where the Barbary states of North Africa had always made much of their living from plundering European shipping, piracy was still as much a hazard as always. Any triangular-shaped sail on the horizon could be a Moorish corsair, lateen-rigged and fast, ready to shoot away spars, then board in overwhelming force.

Many governments (such as those of England, France, and the new United States of America) found it cheapest just to pay extortion to the local emir or caliph to ensure that they would not capture their merchant ships, or hold their people hostage for ransom, or sell them into slavery. Not until the great peace following the Napoleonic wars in 1815 were the western powers able to deploy the naval force needed to control the Mediterranean.

The same period of widespread peace also put the European privateers out of business once and for all. Without a war, there was no more excuse for privateers, no further profit, and, in the new world order, this time there was nowhere for them to turn. Inevitably, the occasional freelance pirates cropped up here or there, usually a handful of villainous mutineers taking over a little vessel, killing its master and any crew who would not join them, then going on a murderous rampage among local shipping until caught and hanged. Their careers seldom lasted more than a few weeks.

There were some exceptions who were more dangerous. A few professional sea thugs still operated from Cuba and other Caribbean islands that had safe hidey-holes for their fast schooners. These are remembered as history's most vicious pirates of all, far exceeding their forebears in sheer cruelty, inflicting gruesome tortures on their captives; these men, women, and children were to be murdered, so no one of them would ever give testimony in any Admiralty court.

The pirate lairs were mostly destroyed in the 1820s by the new American Navy, but others sprang up elsewhere around South America as that conti-nent's wars of independence played out. These bred more privateers, who carried on afterward on their own account into the 1830s, again with great savagery. Perhaps the most notorious of these was Benito de Soto, whose clipper-built brigantine was named *Black Joke.* A terrifying near-encounter with it, or a brigantine just like it, was described by the famed author and sailor Richard Henry Dana in his classic *Two Years Before the Mast.* Off the coast of Brazil, in very light wind: "We saw a small clipper-built brig with a black hull heading directly after us. We went to work immediately, and put all the canvas [up] which we could get upon her . . ." Extra sails were rigged out, and every trick used to milk more speed from *Pilgrim*, an unarmed, laden merchantman bound for California by way of Cape Horn. "The vessel continued in pursuit, changing her course as we changed ours, to keep before the wind. The captain, who watched her with his glass, said that she was armed, and full of men, and showed no colors.

We continued running dead before the wind, knowing that we sailed better so, and that clippers are fastest on the wind."

The chase went on. They well knew their lives depended upon every yard they could gain. "All hands remained on deck throughout the day, and we got our fire-arms in order; but we were too few to have done anything with her, if she had proved to be what we feared. Fortunately there was no moon, and the night which followed was exceedingly dark, so that, by putting out all the lights on board and altering our course four points, we hoped to get out of her reach. We removed the light in the binnacle, and steered by the stars, and kept perfect silence through the night. At daybreak there was no sign of anything in the horizon . . ."

Dana escaped to become the first powerful advocate for sailors' rights; de Soto was caught and hanged. Both events marked the last era of the great age of sail. Pirates, of course, remained. Pirates have been here from time before memory . . . and here they are still.

ARTIST'S EPILOGUE

All of this book's pictures are fictions except for one. It's true that they have all been closely researched for accuracy as to every known historical detail, but, inescapably, this illustrator had to imagine every scene, like all the other pirate illustrators, even those of the pirates' own time.

The exception came to me on a passage that I made, not too long ago, between Nassau and Jamaica by way of Cuba, aboard an ancient gaff-rigged cutter. It had been chartered by a magazine to retrace Calico Jack Rackham's route between those islands on his last voyage with Anne Bonny and Mary Read, and I had been hired to advise. Our old vessel had a crew of three freelance Caribbean hands. All had nicknames that were well known among the community of well-educated sailors who eke out their independence in those tropical waters by following whatever opportunities come their way – in this case, a charter.

At the time, I was aware that at least two of the crew had been convicted and punished for smuggling, and that the rules by which they were guided were shaped according to their own lights. But they did know how to sail their old boat, and they brought a color to the project that fit it well.

I had sailed with them for almost a week, seeing them every day without seeing them as members of the modern-day brotherhood of the coast. But then I did, one night in the Windward Passage. I came out of the hatch to a sky that was brilliantly illuminated by moon, stars, and reflective clouds, towering, as clouds do, over those waters. The wake hissed, the spars creaked, the rum was to hand. The conversation was philosophical at first, something to do with the transience of mortality; after that there was the more practical subject of what kind of Cuban cigars to buy in Santiago and sell somewhere else without the formality of legal Customs documents.

I made a sketch on the spot, by the light of a small flashlight that I held in my teeth, beginning the process of making a picture that was at last no fiction. It would have been harder by the light of an oil lantern, as in former times, but the cast of characters had not changed, nor the moon, nor the dark seas sliding under us.

FURTHER READING

All readers who have enjoyed this book should be aware that it is a picture sequel to William Gilkerson's previous book on the same subject, the Governor General's Award-winning, novel *Pirate's Passage* (Shambhala Publications, 2006).

For further reading on the general subject, the author recommends David Cordingly's factual history *Life Among the Pirates* and its companion picture book, *Pirates: Fact and Fiction,* by David Cordingly and John Falconer. Cordingly has also written the commentary for a new edition of the most authentic of all contemporary pirate histories, Captain Charles Johnson's 1724 *A General History of the Robberies & Murders of the Most Notorious Pirates.* Many insights into the same period of history are found in Marcus Rediker's *Between the Devil and the Deep Blue Sea.*

For readers who want to know more about piracy's earlier eras, Peter Earle's *The Sack of Panama* offers a vivid look at Morgan's time, and Robert C. Ritchie's *Captain Kidd and the War Against the Pirates* does the same for Kidd's period. The single best contemporary account of the buccaneers is Alexandre Olivier Esquemeling's *Boucaniers of America,* first published in 1678. A first-hand of privateering can be found in Woodes Rogers's journal of 1712, titled *A Cruising Voyage Round the World.* Various reprints of both have been published over the years, as with *The Journal of Bernal Diaz,* a conquistador's eyewitness account of Mexico's invasion by Cortez in 1519. Readers might find this more easily in the modern edition *The Conquest of New Spain* by Bernal Diaz del Castillo.

Those who want to know more about Granuaile are directed to Anne Chamber's biography *Granuaille: Ireland's Pirate Queen,* and those wanting more on John Paul Jones from William Gilkerson are directed to his written and illustrated history *The Ships of John Paul Jones;* the author cites Samuel Eliot Morison's *John Paul Jones: A Sailor's Biography* as the best scholarly Jones biography, and the most readable.

Richard Henry Dana's *Two Years Before the Mast,* quoted in the final chapter here, gives a profoundly compelling account of a common sailor's shipboard life in the nineteenth century.

And for all readers who want to look at more pictures of pirates, the author recommends the work of the great American illustrator N. C. Wyeth in the 1911 Scribners edition of Robert Louis Stevenson's *Treasure Island* (recently reissued), and the work of Howard Pyle in the Harper & Brothers 1921 classic *Howard Pyle's Book of Pirates* (also recently reissued).

ACKNOWLEDGMENTS

The author's thanks go George Dawson for assistance with laying out the maps; to Karl Rosenberger for the original commission that led to this book's illustrations, and to the three museums that ultimately featured them in their exhibit *Under the Black Flag*, which traveled from New York's South Street Seaport Museum to the Mariner's Museum at Newport News, Virginia., to Philadelphia's Independence Seaport Museum.

Thanks also go to the United States Naval Academy Museum, the Beverley R. Robinson Collection, and the Naval Institute Press, who jointly published my illustrated history *The Ships of John Paul Jones*, in which all of Chapter Nine's pictures were originally published.

Lastly, and with great heart, my thanks go to those individuals without whom this book would not exist, beginning with the staff at Tundra Books, publisher. A several-gun salute goes to Janet Joy Wilson; and, first and last and always, to my front-line editor, secretary, caregiver, and wife—Kerstin, to whom all of my work is dedicated, piratical and otherwise.

INDEX

ARCTIC SEAS

BERING SEA

SEA of OKHOTSK

SEA of JAPAN

YELLOW SEA

S. CHINA SEA

40°N

PACIFIC OCEAN

PHILIPPINE SEA

JAVA SEA

TIMOR SEA

CORAL SEA

AUSTRALIAN BIGHT

40°S

GREAT SOUTHERN